D0772644

KYRGYZSTAN

KYRGYZSTAN

Prepared by
Geography Department

Lerner Publications Company
Minneapolis

Series editors: Mary M. Rodgers, Tom Streissguth,
    Colleen Sexton
Photo researcher: Kathy Raskob
Designer: Zachary Marell

Our thanks to the following for their help in preparing
and checking the text of this book: Dr. Craig ZumBrunnen,
Department of Geography, University of Washington;
Dr. Larry Moses, Department of Uralic and Altaic Studies,
Indiana University; Kathleen Kuehnast, Department of
Anthropology, University of Minnesota.

Terms in **bold** appear in a glossary that starts on page 52.

Pronunciation Guide

Akaev	ah-KAH-yev
Birlik	bihr-LUK
Genghis	GEN-giss
glasnost	GLAZ-nost
Issyk-Kul	IHZ-ik—kuhl
Kyrgyzstan	kur-gihz-STAHN
Kyzyl Kiya	KIHZ-il KEE-yah
Manas	mah-NAHS
mosque	MAHSK
muezzin	moo-EZ-in
Naryn	NAH-rihn
Osh	OHSH
perestroika	pehr-eh-STROY-kah
Pobeda	pah-BEE-dah
Uighur	WEE-guhr

LIBRARY OF CONGRESS CATALOGING-IN-PUBLICATION DATA

Kyrgyzstan / prepared by Geography Department, Lerner Publica-
tions Company.
      p.   cm.—(Then & now)
   Includes index.
   Summary: Discusses the history, topography, ethnic mixture,
politics, economics, and future of the former Soviet republic.
   ISBN 0-8225-2814-2 (lib. bdg.)
   1. Kyrgyzstan—Juvenile literature. [1. Kyrgyzstan.] I. Lerner
Publications Company. Geography Dept. II. Series: Then & now
(Minneapolis, Minn.)
DK913.K97 1993
958'.43—dc20   93-12332
                                                    CIP
                                                    AC

• CONTENTS •

In the ancient city of Osh in southern Kyrgyzstan, vendors display fresh loaves of bread at a bazaar (outdoor market).

"We have so many good slogans, but we must translate them into life."

Taabaldy Agemberdiyev,
Member, Democratic Kyrgyzstan

I n 1992, the Soviet Union would have celebrated the 75th anniversary of the revolution of 1917. During that revolt, political activists called **Communists** overthrew the czar (ruler) and the government of the **Russian Empire.** The revolution of 1917 was the first step in establishing the 15-member **Union of Soviet Socialist Republics (USSR).**

The Soviet Union stretched from eastern Europe across northern and central Asia and contained nearly 300 million people. Within this vast nation, the Communist government guaranteed housing, education, health care, and lifetime employment. Communist leaders told farmers and factory workers that Soviet citizens owned all property in common. The new nation quickly **industrialized**, meaning it built many new factories and upgraded existing ones. It also modernized and enlarged its farms. In addition, the USSR created a huge, well-equipped military force that allowed it to become one of the most powerful nations in the world.

In a town along Kyrgyzstan's border with Kazakhstan, a large billboard shows flags from the 15 republics of the old Soviet Union.

An illustration from Manas, *the Kyrgyz national epic, shows warriors battling in defense of their homeland.*

In Bishkek, a Russian gymnast trains on the rings, which are hung from two parallel straps. During ring routines, athletes combine stationary positions with rapid movements to show strength and precision.

Kyrgyzstan—a remote, mountainous republic in central Asia—was brought into the Soviet Union in the 1920s. Most **ethnic Kyrgyz** herded animals and grew crops only in a few isolated valleys. Nevertheless, Soviet leaders developed new industries and mines in the region, and workers from Russia and Ukraine settled in Kyrgyzstan. The republic's rapid modernization improved living standards but also led to political and ethnic tensions, which worsened throughout central Asia during the 1980s.

Factories in Osh produce fine silk fabric from the cocoons (outer coverings) of silkworms. Here, a worker dips cocoons in hot water to loosen the silk threads that will later be wound onto a reel.

By the early 1990s, the Soviet Union was in a period of rapid change and turmoil. The central government had mismanaged the economy, which was failing to provide goods. To control the various ethnic groups within the USSR, the Communists had long restricted many freedoms. People throughout the vast nation were dissatisfied.

Several of the republics were seeking independence from Soviet rule—a development that worried some old-style Communists. In August 1991, these conservative Communists tried to use Soviet military power to overthrow the nation's president in a **coup d'état.** Their effort failed and hastened the breakup of the USSR.

At the same time, Kyrgyzstan was experiencing a coup attempt against its own president, Askar Akaev. The coup failed, leading Akaev to ban Kyrgyzstan's Communist party and to form a democratic government. Kyrgyzstan declared its independence in October 1991 and later joined the **Commonwealth of Independent States,** an association of former Soviet republics.

Kyrgyzstan, like its central Asian neighbors, now faces severe economic and social problems as it adjusts to independence. Long dependent on Soviet investment in industry and on trade with other Soviet republics, Kyrgyzstan must develop a self-reliant economy. The country suffers from a lack of arable (fertile) land and obsolete factories. In addition, Kyrgyzstan has experienced violence among its various ethnic groups.

Nevertheless, Kyrgyzstan has a relatively stable government, and rival political parties are working together in the Kyrgyz parliament. In addition, Kyrgyz leaders are seeking trade agreements with neighboring countries. If successful, these new ties may improve Kyrgyzstan's economy and raise the standard of living for all the country's citizens.

CHAPTER ONE

The Land and People of Kyrgyzstan

Manas, the ancient epic of the Kyrgyz people, tells of the fierce struggle of the warrior Manas and the Kyrgyz for a free and independent life. In 1991, this dream became a reality after the breakup of the Soviet Union. Within a year, the Kyrgyz had declared their independence, and the new nation of Kyrgyzstan had become a member of the **United Nations.**

Despite its newfound freedom, Kyrgyzstan is still beset by problems. A landlocked nation that is mountainous and isolated, Kyrgyzstan suffered turmoil and violence as the Soviet Union dissolved. Many of the Kyrgyz are poor, and the nation's economy is still largely based on livestock herding and crop growing. Nevertheless, Kyrgyzstan is self-sufficient in food, and the Kyrgyz may benefit from foreign trade with the other newly independent republics of central Asia.

The towering peaks of the Pamir-Alai Mountains dominate southwestern Kyrgyzstan, as well as parts of other former Soviet republics in central Asia. The height of the range has given the region its nickname—"the roof of the world."

(Right) **A Kyrgyz farmer guides his horse through the foothills of the Tien Mountains, which lie along Kyrgyzstan's border with China.** (Below) **Streams supply rural Kyrgyz with water for drinking and cooking.**

• The Lay of the Land •

The Republic of Kyrgyzstan is located high in the mountains of central Asia, an area sometimes called the "roof of the world." Kyrgyzstan shares long, winding borders to the west with Uzbekistan and to the west and south with Tajikistan. Kazakhstan lies in the north, and China is Kyrgyzstan's eastern neighbor. Kyrgyzstan covers 76,500 square miles (198,135 square kilometers), an area roughly the size of South Dakota or twice the size of Portugal.

Mountain ranges define many of Kyrgyzstan's twisting borders. Most of the country lies more than 5,000 feet (1,500 meters) above sea level. At least 75 percent of the land is covered by permafrost, meaning that the ground never completely thaws, even during the summer. Short and rapid mountain streams feed about 3,000 lakes that dot the landscape.

Kyrgyzstan's highlands fall into several distinct regions. One system, the Tien Mountains, crosses Kyrgyzstan from southwest to northeast along the Chinese border. Within this range rise two of the tallest peaks in central Asia—Mount Pobeda, which reaches 24,400 feet (7,440 m), and the 22,950-foot (6,995-m) Khan-Tengri, which straddles the border with Kazakhstan. In the southwest are the Pamir-Alai Mountains, which reach more than 23,000 feet (7,000 m). Glaciers (slow-moving ice masses) and snow cover the high elevations for much of the year, and earthquakes often strike central and eastern Kyrgyzstan.

A few isolated lowlands exist along Kyrgyzstan's western and northern borders. In the southwest is the fertile Fergana Valley, which Kyrgyzstan shares with Uzbekistan and Tajikistan. The site of extensive pastures and numerous farms and towns, the Fergana Valley receives most of its water from streams that flow into it from the surrounding mountains. Along Kyrgyzstan's frontier with Kazakhstan are the valleys of the Chu and Talas rivers. These densely populated valleys also include many farms, villages, and small cities.

• Waterways, Lakes, and Glaciers •

Most of Kyrgyzstan's rivers begin in the mountains and flow into low-lying basins in neighboring nations. The rapid currents of these rivers are ideal for the generation of hydroelectric power, as well as for the irrigation of crops growing at lower elevations.

Erosion by wind and water has shaped these rock formations in a Kyrgyz valley.

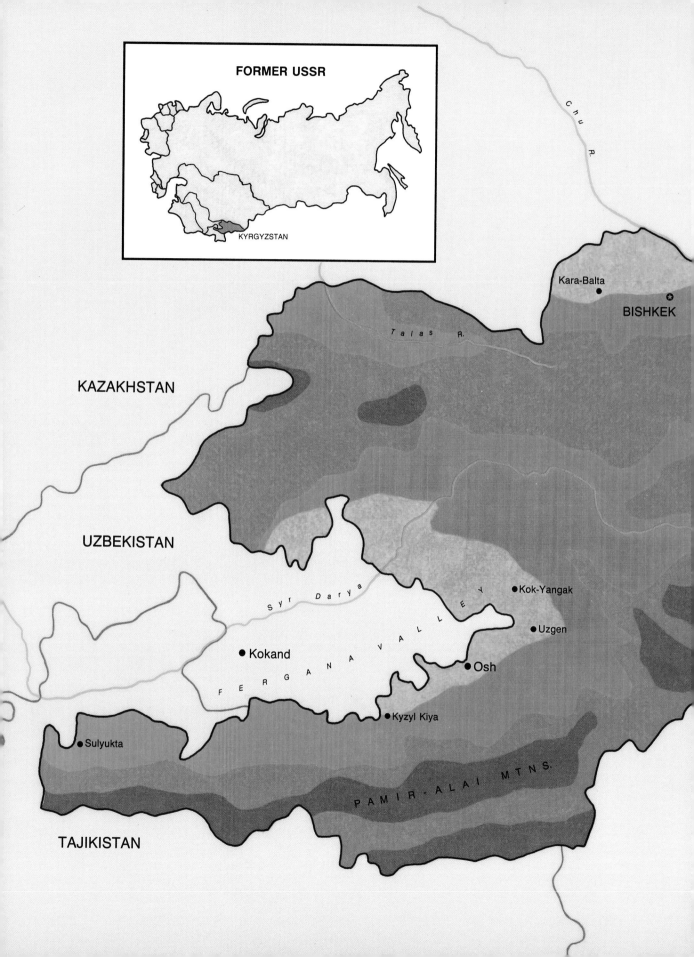

FORMER USSR

KYRGYZSTAN

Chu R.

Kara-Balta

★ BISHKEK

Talas R.

KAZAKHSTAN

UZBEKISTAN

Syr Darya

Kok-Yangak

Uzgen

F E R G A N A   V A L L E Y

Kokand

Osh

Kyzyl Kiya

Sulyukta

P A M I R - A L A I   M T N S.

TAJIKISTAN

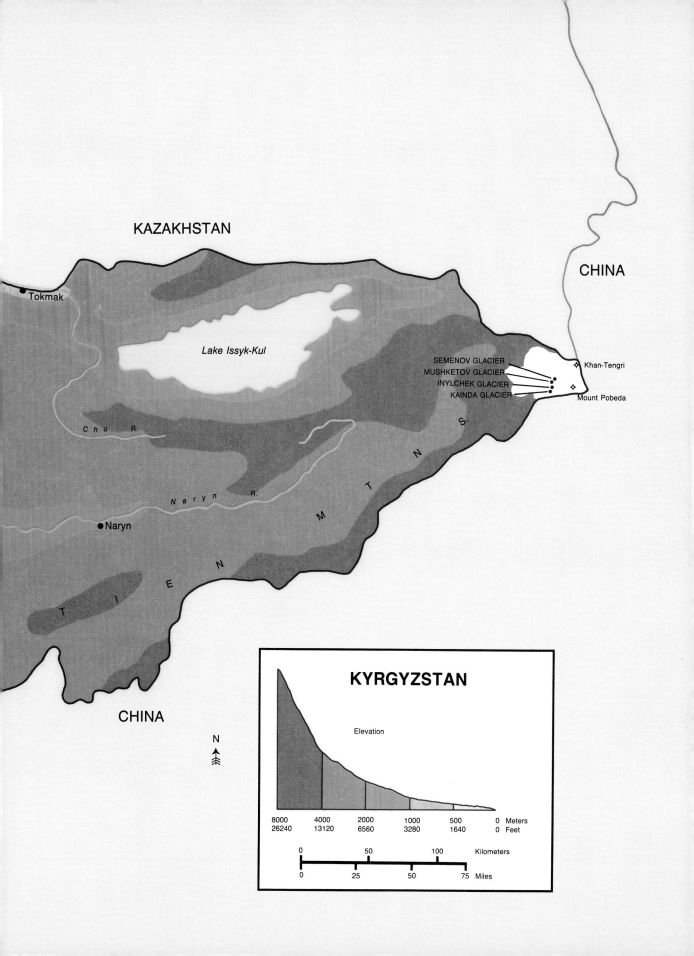

KAZAKHSTAN

CHINA

Tokmak

Lake Issyk-Kul

SEMENOV GLACIER
MUSHKETOV GLACIER
INYLCHEK GLACIER
KAINDA GLACIER

Khan-Tengri

Mount Pobeda

C h u R.

N a r y n R.

Naryn

T I E N

M T N S.

T I E N   S H A N

CHINA

N

KYRGYZSTAN

Elevation

| 8000 | 4000 | 2000 | 1000 | 500 | 0 | Meters |
| 26240 | 13120 | 6560 | 3280 | 1640 | 0 | Feet |

| 0 | | 50 | | 100 | Kilometers |

| 0 | 25 | 50 | 75 | Miles |

The largest waterway in Kyrgyzstan is the Naryn River, which rises in the northeast and travels westward. The Naryn and several other streams feed the Syr Darya (River), which crosses the Fergana Valley and empties into the Aral Sea in Kazakhstan. Many small tributaries along Kyrgyzstan's northern border join to form the Chu and Talas rivers. These waterways run northward into the deserts of Kazakhstan, where they evaporate. In the east and southeast, Kyrgyzstan's small mountain streams flow eastward into China.

Although there are about 3,000 lakes in Kyrgyzstan, most of them are quite small. The country's largest body of water is Lake Issyk-Kul, a salt lake that fills a highland basin in the northeast. Lake

Along the shore of Lake Issyk-Kul, women wash a sheepskin before letting it dry. Covering an area of 2,355 square miles (6,099 square kilometers), the blue lake sits high in the Tien range and is fed by dozens of mountain streams.

Issyk-Kul's abundant stocks of fish support several fishing villages.

Glaciers cover about 3 percent of Kyrgyzstan, and most of them lie in the east near the Chinese border. Kyrgyzstan has some of the world's longest glaciers, including the Inylchek Glacier—which is 32 miles (51 km) long—and the Kainda, Semenov, and Mushketov glaciers. Avalanches and earthquakes cause constant shifting within these glacier fields.

• *Climate* •

Kyrgyzstan's climate is entirely free of seaborne winds and storm systems, and the country's high

(Above) *Friends fish the waters of the Chu River, which crosses Kyrgyzstan's border with Kazakhstan.* (Right) *Skiers navigate a steep glacier in the Pamir-Alai Mountains.*

mountains block the winds that regularly bring rain to southern Asia. Temperatures in Kyrgyzstan range from warm to bitterly cold, and precipitation varies greatly depending on altitude. Most of the country has between 150 to 200 days of sunshine each year.

At the lower elevations in the west, winds from the deserts of central Asia bring hot, dry air in the summer and cold, dry air in the winter. July temperatures may average 80°F (26°C) in the valleys, while January temperatures average about –1°F (–18°C). In the capital city of Bishkek, in northern Kyrgyzstan, temperatures range from highs of 104°F (40°C) in July to lows of –40°F (–40°C) in January.

At high elevations, temperature ranges are much greater. Above 10,000 feet (3,000 m), temperatures in July average about 40°F (5°C), and in January about –18°F (–27°C). A record low of –65°F (–54°C) has been reached in the mountains. The amount of rain and snow depends on the direction from which the precipitation is coming. Annual precipitation varies from 2 inches (5 centimeters) on slopes facing north to as much as 30 inches (76 cm) in the highlands facing the Fergana Valley. The highest mountains receive little precipitation, mostly as snow. The snow gathers gradually to form glaciers. Melting glaciers provide water to streams that irrigate the dry mountain valleys.

• Cities •

About 40 percent of Kyrgyzstan's 4.5 million people live in cities or towns. Bishkek, the nation's only large city, has a population of 634,000. This city was called Pishpek until 1925, when Soviet authorities renamed it Frunze to honor the Russian revolutionary leader Mikhail Frunze, who was born in Pishpek in 1885. After 1991, the city's name

(Above) **Bishkek's racecourse draws large crowds, even during a driving rain.** (Below) **This tall clock tower—a Bishkek landmark—rises above the capital's main telephone office.**

In Osh, a muezzin (Islamic crier)
uses a public-address system to
call Muslims (followers of Islam)
to prayer.

became Bishkek. Located in the Chu River Valley, Bishkek serves as an administrative center as well as a hub of higher education. Bishkek's factories make leather goods, agricultural machinery, and textiles.

Founded along the **Silk Road**—a famous trade route that passed through central Asia—Bishkek grew rapidly after its conquest by the Russian Empire in 1862. A new railroad connected the town to the rest of the empire, and immigrants soon began arriving from Russia and Ukraine. **Ethnic Russians** and **ethnic Ukrainians** still make up a majority of Bishkek's population.

The oldest urban settlement in Kyrgyzstan is the ancient city of Osh, which dates to the 3rd century B.C. Located in the foothills of the Pamir-Alai Mountains, Osh has a population of about 180,000. For much of its early history, it was an important caravan station on the Silk Road. The city still has a silk industry and processes cotton and other agricultural products.

While Kyrgyzstan was part of the Soviet Union, many other smaller cities were built as centers for mining and manufacturing. These towns—most of which have fewer than 100,000 inhabitants—include Kara-Balta, Kok-Yangak, Kyzyl Kiya, Sulyukta, and Naryn. In the near future, the Russian names of many cities in Kyrgyzstan may be changed to Kyrgyz names.

• *Ethnic Heritage* •

The first mention of a Kyrgyz people living in Kyrgyzstan appears in Arab and Persian documents of the early 16th century. After leaving their homes in the Yenisei River Valley of Siberia, in what is now eastern Russia, the Kyrgyz gradually took control of the high valleys of the Tien and Pamir-Alai ranges.

The newcomers were often at war with their neighbors and with each other and occasionally came under the rule of more powerful states. As a result of invasions and migrations, modern Kyrgyz culture and language show the influence of many different ethnic groups.

Ethnic Kyrgyz make up about 49 percent of the nation's population. Kyrgyz also inhabit Uzbekistan, China, and Afghanistan, a nation lying south of Tajikistan. The Kyrgyz, most of whom are agricultural workers and herders, live in villages at higher elevations in the north and east. Only about 20 percent of the nation's ethnic Kyrgyz reside in urban areas and hold industrial or professional jobs.

Slavs—mostly Russians and Ukrainians—make up about 24 percent of the country's population. These peoples began arriving in Kyrgyzstan in the late 19th century, when Kyrgyzstan became part of the Russian Empire. They settled mainly in northern Kyrgyzstan, in Bishkek, and in the Chu and Fergana valleys. A majority of Russians and Ukrainians still live in Kyrgyzstan's urban areas. In spite of Kyrgyzstan's independence, most ethnic Slavs have chosen to remain in the country.

Ethnic Germans number about 100,000. Like several other ethnic groups, Germans settled in the region during World War II (1939–1945) after being forced from their homes in Russia. The Uighurs are a Turkish people who live in Kyrgyzstan, as well as in western China. Smaller groups of Tatars, Chinese, and Tajiks complete the country's ethnic mixture.

Kyrgyz newlyweds pause for a photo in a sheep pasture.

At this day-care center in Bishkek, a teacher instructs her
young students in both Russian
and Kyrgyz.

• Religion •

Most Kyrgyz follow the religion of Islam, which was founded by the Arab prophet Muhammad in the 7th century A.D. This faith was introduced in southern Kyrgyzstan after the Arab invasion of central Asia in the 8th century. Because of the high mountain barrier that prevented communication across central Kyrgyzstan, Islam arrived in northern Kyrgyzstan much later—as recently as the 18th century, according to some scholars.

Islam became an important element in Kyrgyz life and culture. One of the most holy Islamic shrines was built in the city of Osh. In the 20th century, however, the Soviet government outlawed religious practices and education and closed the country's mosques (Islamic houses of prayer) and madrasas (religious schools). After Kyrgyzstan gained its

Since gaining independence in 1991, Kyrgyzstan has lifted religious restrictions imposed by the old Soviet regime. The country's Russian population attends services in Orthodox Christian churches (left), *while Kyrgyz Muslims pray at Islamic mosques* (right).

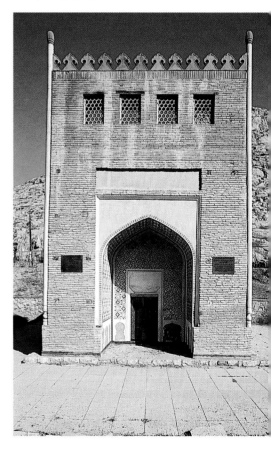

independence, the new government lifted these restrictions. Kyrgyz Muslims (followers of Islam) are reopening or restoring mosques, and Muslim leaders are once again teaching the laws and prayers of the faith. Most Kyrgyz view Islam as a social rather than as a spiritual force in their culture, and Kyrgyzstan will probably maintain a secular (nonreligious) government.

Like other central Asian peoples, the Kyrgyz belong to the Sunni branch of Islam rather than to the Shiite sect common in Iran and Azerbaijan. The two sects divided centuries ago over Islam's leadership. Shiite Muslims accept only leaders descended from Muhammad's family, while Sunni leaders are not necessarily related to the prophet. Another sect of Islam, known as **Sufism**, is popular among the Kyrgyz. Sufi brotherhoods, which are growing in popularity in southern Kyrgyzstan, teach a more mystical form of Islam.

Using lettering in both Arabic (top) and Cyrillic (bottom), a sign over the door of a mosque in Bishkek welcomes visitors. The new Kyrgyz government is introducing the Latin alphabet to write Kyrgyz and is planning to use the Kyrgyz language in many public schools.

Slavic peoples living in Kyrgyzstan practice Orthodox Christianity, which has long been the religion of Russians and Ukrainians. Although the Soviets also suppressed this faith, Orthodox Christianity survived in the republics of central Asia. Other Christian denominations in Kyrgyzstan include Lutheranism, a Protestant sect followed by the country's Germans. Ethnic Chinese living in Kyrgyzstan practice Buddhism.

• Language, Education, and Health •

Kyrgyz is one of many Turkic languages—which include Kazakh and Uzbek—used within the former USSR. Modern Kyrgyz is spoken by about 2.5 million people in Kyrgyzstan, China, Afghanistan, Tajikistan, and Uzbekistan. Although the language has several dialects, most Kyrgyz-speakers can easily understand each other.

Before the Communist revolution of 1917, there was little formal education in Kyrgyzstan. Most schools were madrasas that taught Islamic subjects, as well as the Arabic language. In the 1800s and early 1900s, the Russians founded a few nonreligious schools that enrolled Russian children and a small number of Kyrgyz. According to Russian estimates, however, only 1 percent of all Kyrgyz were literate in 1917.

After the founding of the USSR, all religious schools were closed. The Soviet government required children to attend public schools, and teaching at all levels was in Russian. The Soviets replaced the Arabic lettering used for Kyrgyz with the Latin alphabet and later with Cyrillic, the alphabet used for Russian and Ukrainian. By the early 1990s, about 90 percent of all ethnic Kyrgyz could read and write either Kyrgyz or Russian.

At an elementary school in the capital, students rush to their classrooms.

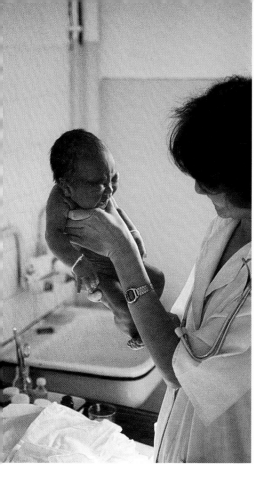

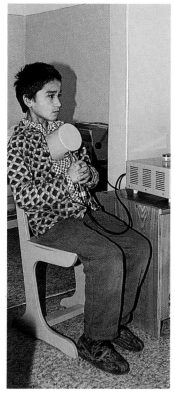

(Left) **A nurse soothes a crying newborn at a maternity hospital in Bishkek.** (Below) **In Osh, a young patient receives a cardiograph, a test that records movements of the heart.**

Under Soviet rule, fluency in Russian was necessary for admission to a university and for success in scientific and technical careers. In addition, nearly all textbooks were printed in Russian. After Kyrgyzstan won its independence, the Kyrgyz language returned to the classroom, although Russian is still used to teach technical subjects, such as engineering. In addition, the Kyrgyz government is replacing Cyrillic with the Latin alphabet.

Students attend seven to nine years of primary school, and two or three years of secondary school. Vocational schools offer two-year programs. Post-secondary education is available for promising students, either at institutes in Kyrgyzstan or in other former Soviet republics. Several Turkish schools have been established, and students attending these schools have the right to enter universities in Turkey, a rapidly modernizing nation in the Middle East.

The Soviet government also built new hospitals and clinics in Kyrgyzstan, although these mostly benefited urban residents. Rural Kyrgyz still suffer high rates of disease and poor living standards. In addition, Kyrgyzstan's population is growing by 2.2 percent a year, a rapid rate that will double the number of inhabitants in 31 years. Infant mortality—the number of babies who die within a year of their birth—stands at 35 per 1,000. This is the lowest rate among the former Soviet republics of central Asia and is roughly equal to that of China. Life expectancy in Kyrgyzstan is 68 years.

CHAPTER TWO

Kyrgyzstan's Story

A ncient cave paintings, rock carvings, and tools reveal that humans inhabited Kyrgyzstan as early as 300,000 years ago. Other archaeological finds show that Kyrgyzstan suffered many invasions from the east and south. During the Neolithic era (7000 to 3000 B.C.), farmers were tending crops and cattle in Kyrgyzstan's river valleys and near the shores of Lake Issyk-Kul. About 3000 B.C., traders began crossing Kyrgyzstan's steep mountain ranges, which lay between China and the rest of central Asia.

As a result of wars to the east in Mongolia, groups of nomadic herders and hunters began migrating into central Asia as early as the 3rd century B.C. Some chose to remain in Kyrgyzstan, while others continued into India, western Asia, or eastern Europe. At the same time, groups already established in Kyrgyzstan were forming alliances with one another and with foreign states.

Elaborate brickwork decorates the 12th-century Burana Tower in Tokmak, a city in northern Kyrgyzstan that is known for its production of glass and wool.

In the 1st century A.D., the people of southern Kyrgyzstan were conquered by the Kushan Empire, a realm based in what is now Afghanistan. Kushan leaders built new irrigation canals that channeled the mountain streams to cultivated fields. The Kushan realm also benefited from trade along the Silk Road, which passed through ancient Osh. In northern Kyrgyzstan, many nomadic peoples were settling in the river valleys to raise grain and livestock.

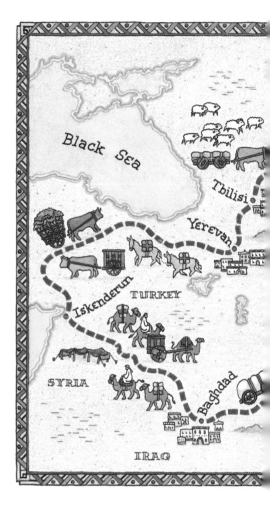

• *Turkic Principalities* •

In the 6th and 7th centuries A.D., Turkic peoples invaded from the east and established the West Turkic kaganate (principality), with its capital in Kyrgyzstan's Chu River Valley. This state was a part of the vast Turkic Empire of Mongolia. After the establishment of the kaganate, the population of Kyrgyzstan adopted Turkic languages.

The Turkic inhabitants of the kaganate founded many new towns in the river valleys, where merchants traded cotton, leather, and food for livestock raised by mountain herders. The Chu River Valley was located along the busy Silk Road, which linked China, the Middle East, and Europe. After the Arab invasions of the 8th century A.D., traders and missionaries traveling along the Silk Road brought the religion of Islam to the people of southern Kyrgyzstan.

Beginning in the 10th century, Kyrgyzstan's economy grew rapidly. Miners in the Talas River Valley extracted valuable silver ore, and new cities developed along the shores of Lake Issyk-Kul and in northern Kyrgyzstan. The kaganate's leaders raised impressive monuments in the cities, which flourished from the trade in agricultural goods, minerals, and handicrafts.

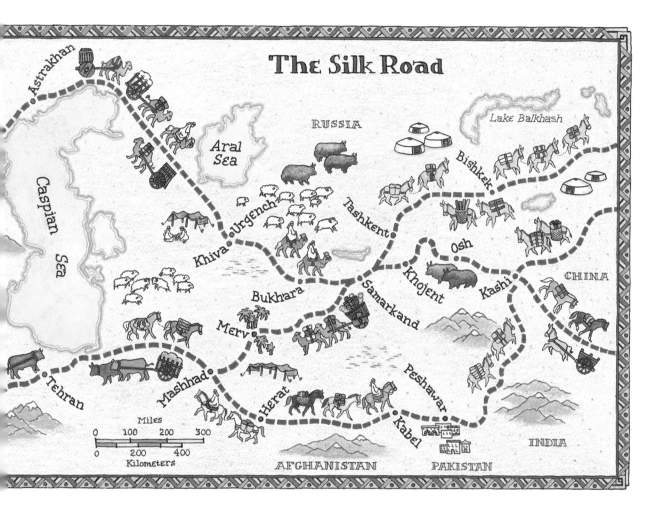

The Silk Road

Linking China and Europe, the 4,000-mile (6,400-km) Silk Road thrived beginning in the 2nd century B.C. Caravans brought fine silk fabric westward, while horses, glass, wool, gold, and silver made the journey eastward. Few merchants traveled the entire route. Instead, drivers used camels, oxen, donkeys, and horses to move goods from city to city. Local brokers in Osh and elsewhere helped to find buyers for the bolts of cloth and other valuable merchandise.

As early as the 12th century, a people known as the Kyrgyz began moving from Siberia—a region to the north—into the Tien Mountains. The Kyrgyz bands were headed by **manaps,** who claimed descent from ancient chiefs. At this time, Chinese, Turkic, and Arab peoples were fighting for control of trade and of Kyrgyzstan's fertile river valleys.

• Mongol Invasions •

In the 13th century, an invasion of Mongol warriors under their leader Genghis Khan devastated Kyrgyzstan. Mounted on horseback, the Mongols

The 12th-century Mongol commander Genghis Khan led his armies through central Asia, where they destroyed cities and farms.

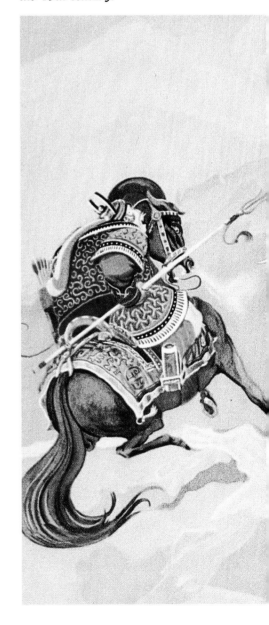

Warriors clash in a drawing from Manas. Originally sung or recited, the story consists of about 500,000 lines in verse form and has been passed from generation to generation since the 15th century.

destroyed towns, farms, and irrigation systems. The attacks forced many inhabitants of Kyrgyzstan to abandon their settled way of life and to become nomadic herders.

After the Mongol invasion, Kyrgyzstan splintered into several small states. Based in the region's river valleys, these domains were isolated from one another by the high mountain ranges. In the late 15th century, several Kyrgyz bands united to form a khanate (realm of a khan or prince) in northern Kyrgyzstan. The people of the Kyrgyz khanate made their living from cattle herding, crop growing, and caravan trade.

The khanate faced enemies along all its borders. The most dangerous were the Oirat Mongols to the east. From the 1680s to the 1750s, the Oirat staged repeated raids on Kyrgyz lands. Although the Kyrgyz eventually defeated the Oirat, the khanate was badly weakened by the conflict. The Kyrgyz were unable to defend themselves against the khans of Kokand, a city in what is now Uzbekistan.

By the end of the 18th century, the Kokandian khanate succeeded in subduing the Kyrgyz and in seizing Kyrgyz territory. To police the region, Kokand's rulers built fortresses in Tokmak and in Pishpek (modern Bishkek), towns in the Chu River Valley.

• *The Russian Empire* •

The rule of the Kokandian khans proved harsh. In the early 19th century, frequent rebellions against Kokand broke out among the Kyrgyz. Meanwhile, the Russian Empire was expanding into central Asia. The Russian czar (ruler) sought control of trade routes to China and India that passed through the mountains and deserts of central Asia. By the 1860s, many of the Kyrgyz groups who wanted independence from Kokand had allied with Russia.

Between 1855 and 1876, Russian armies conquered the Kokandian khanate and gradually took control of most of Kyrgyzstan—a region known to the Russians as Kirghizia. The empire built new mining and manufacturing operations in Kirghizia, which became part of **Russian Turkestan**, a province of the Russian Empire. Trade in industrial goods, food, and cotton increased, and the population of the region grew quickly as immigrants arrived from Russia and Ukraine.

The czar's government gave Russian and Ukrainian farmers who settled in Kirghizia the best farmland in the lower mountain valleys. This action put the settlers in conflict with Kyrgyz cattle herders who used these valleys for pasture. Between 1866 and 1916, Russian immigration drove many Kyrgyz from the lowlands into the higher elevations, where the soils are less fertile and the climate is more harsh. As a result of these conditions, the Kyrgyz herders became poorer, and their herds declined in size.

A statue in Bishkek honors the Communist revolution of 1917, which toppled the Russian Empire and led to the founding of the Soviet Union.

The Russian Empire took over Kyrgyz lands in the 19th century, giving the best parts of the territory to Russian settlers. This policy forced traditional Kyrgyz herders, such as this yak farmer, to move to higher and less fertile ground.

• World War I and Revolution •

In the early 1900s, dissatisfaction among the Kyrgyz increased. At the same time, the Russian Empire was suffering widespread unrest among its workers and farm laborers. The situation worsened as the czar's forces suffered a disastrous defeat during World War I (1914–1918), a conflict fought among the European powers. The Russian government heavily taxed Kirghizia and drafted many Kyrgyz into the Russian army. In addition, Kyrgyz farmers were forced to turn over their crops and livestock to feed soldiers fighting in Europe.

In 1916, central Asia's economic hardship sparked a revolt that spread throughout Turkestan. Thousands of Russians and Kyrgyz were killed in the fighting. To escape the czarist government's harsh repression, as many as 150,000 Kyrgyz fled to China, although most of these refugees later returned.

Although the rebellion in Turkestan was defeated, the Russian government was weakening. Political activists called Communists pushed for the czar's overthrow. In 1917, the Russian Communist party succeeded in toppling the Russian government. Although the Kyrgyz hoped for independence, the Communists instead incorporated Kyrgyz lands into their new state. When a civil war erupted in 1918, many Kyrgyz joined the Basmachi movement, a rebellion that united the people of Turkestan against foreign rule. The Communists eventually defeated the movement, although it survived underground through the 1920s and 1930s.

• Soviet Rule •

In 1922, the Communist party established the Union of Soviet Socialist Republics (USSR). Communist leaders brought Kirghizia and other central

After several years of local rebellion, Communist forces conquered central Asia in the 1920s and added it to the Soviet Union. Posters depicting brave central Asian Communist leaders encouraged the region's many ethnic groups to support Communist ideals. The Soviets eventually created five separate Soviet Socialist Republics (SSRs) in central Asia, one of which was the Kirghiz SSR.

Born in 1885, Mikhail Frunze was a hero of the Communist revolution. Because of his service to the Soviet state, the Communists named the capital of Soviet Kirghizia after him and raised a statue in his honor.

Asian nations into the USSR by reorganizing the territory of Turkestan and by putting local Communist officials in control. In 1926, the Soviets founded the Kirghiz Autonomous Republic. Ten years later, this state became the Kirghiz Soviet Socialist Republic (SSR), with its capital at Frunze (modern Bishkek).

Joseph Stalin, who became the Soviet Union's ruler in 1927, brought several changes to Soviet Kirghizia. His policies were intended to turn the republic into a supplier of raw materials for Soviet industries. State-owned companies dug new mines to extract coal, tin, gold, and other minerals. Stalin extended Soviet control by putting Communists in charge of all aspects of Kyrgyz life.

The Communist party seized all private land and property and transferred it to the government. New laws created **collective farms** by combining many small private holdings into large estates. Farmers became government employees who shared their labor and their earnings with other members of the collectives. To protest these policies, many Kyrgyz killed their animals or fled to China with their herds.

New investment by the Communist government brought some improvement to the republic's economy. The Soviets modernized industries and increased trade. Education, health care, and transportation also improved. But the rapid modernization also brought harm to the environment as new factories and mines polluted the air and water. The Kyrgyz, like other central Asian peoples, lost many of their religious, political, and personal freedoms. During the 1930s, many Kyrgyz leaders who resisted Stalin's policies were executed.

(Above) **A Kyrgyz veteran shows off his military medals from World War II (1939– 1945).** (Below) **Soviet leaders forced Kyrgyz farmers to work on government-owned collective farms, which owed their harvest to the state.**

• *World War II and Its Aftermath* •

The Soviet Union entered World War II, another prolonged international conflict, when Germany invaded the western USSR in 1941. Although it was far from the war front, Soviet Kirghizia was still affected by the fighting. Kyrgyz soldiers served in the Soviet Red Army, while people living in the republic contributed their money, labor, and possessions to the war effort. In addition, the Soviet government moved many heavy industries from the republics of the western USSR to the Kirghiz SSR to prevent destruction by German bombs. During the war, the Soviets also deported to Soviet Kirghizia people suspected of disloyalty—including Germans, Russians, Ukrainians, Tatars, and the Chechen-Ingush.

World War II ended in 1945 with the victory of the Soviet Union and its allies. In the postwar years, Soviet Kirghizia's industries quickly expanded. Mining operations extracted more valuable minerals, including gold, uranium, tin, bauxite, and iron ore. Engineers also discovered deposits of coal, oil, and natural gas. Although living standards improved for city dwellers in the 1960s and 1970s, many ethnic Kyrgyz continued to live in poverty in the countryside and in rural villages.

• *Independence* •

By the 1980s, the USSR was experiencing severe economic and social problems. To improve conditions, Mikhail Gorbachev, who became the Soviet leader in 1985, introduced ***glasnost*** (openness) and ***perestroika*** (restructuring). These policies permitted more open criticism of the Communist government and allowed businesses more freedom to set wages and prices. Although Gorbachev succeeded in making some reforms, the conservative leaders of Soviet Kirghizia strongly opposed the new policies.

Meanwhile, Islam was becoming an important religious and political force in the southern part of the Kirghiz SSR. The ancient city of Osh—the site of an Islamic shrine called Takht-i-Suleiman (the Throne of Suleiman)—became a center of the independence movement. In the late 1980s, public demonstrations took place in Frunze and Osh. In May 1989, Kyrgyz and other central Asian activists founded a group called Birlik (Unity) in Tashkent, Uzbekistan. Members of Birlik organized several large protests against Soviet rule.

Soviet Kirghizia also suffered serious conflicts among its various ethnic groups. In June 1990, more than 200 people died during ethnic clashes between Kyrgyz and Uzbeks in the Fergana Valley. The underlying causes of the violence included competition for housing and segregation according to jobs. Fighting also broke out between Kyrgyz and Tajiks over water rights.

This turmoil led Absamat Masaliev, Soviet Kirghizia's Communist leader, to create the office of president. This official would be elected by members of the republic's government. Soon after this decision, Masaliev's opponents in the legislature formed a new political party called Democratic Kyrgyzstan. Members of this group elected Askar Akaev, a physicist, as their candidate. The legislature later elected Akaev as the republic's first president.

In August 1991, Soviet officials attempted to overthrow Gorbachev in a coup d'état. At the same time, Communists in Soviet Kirghizia staged a similar coup against President Akaev. After the failure of the coup in the Kirghiz SSR, troops loyal to Akaev surrounded the Communist party headquarters in Frunze. After Akaev banned the Kirghiz

(Above) **In Uzgen, a city in the Fergana Valley, a woman reacts to the recent ethnic clashes between the region's Uzbeks and Kyrgyz.** (Below) **Before being named as Kyrgyzstan's president in 1990, Askar Akaev was head of the country's Academy of Sciences. A physicist by training, he has the support of many ex-Communist and democratic politicians.**

Communist party, he was reelected as the republic's president.

The flag of independent Kyrgyzstan, seen here flying over the president's office, features a yellow sun on a red background.

• Recent Events •

The failure of the coup against Gorbachev led to the breakup of the Soviet Union, as the Kirghiz SSR and other Soviet republics declared their independence. The Kirghiz SSR became the Republic of Kyrgyzstan, and the new nation joined Russia, Belarus, Ukraine, and other former Soviet republics as a member of the Commonwealth of Independent States. In March 1992, Kyrgyzstan gained a seat as a full member of the United Nations.

With Islam emerging as the republic's dominant religion, Kyrgyzstan is now developing closer ties with other Muslim countries. The Kyrgyz are also seeking outside investment from Turkey, Korea, and other foreign nations. Kyrgyz leaders have decided to gradually replace the Cyrillic alphabet with Latin lettering, which is used to write modern Turkish. The use of Kyrgyz in public schools and universities, however, may prompt many non-Kyrgyz workers and students to leave.

President Akaev is one of the few leaders in central Asia who is not a former member of the Communist party. For this reason, Kyrgyzstan sometimes suffers strained relations with other central Asian states, whose Communist bosses have remained in power. Kyrgyzstan also is experiencing tension among its ethnic groups, especially in the south, where Kyrgyz compete with Uzbeks, Tajiks, and other peoples for political and economic rights. Since the Kyrgyz economy can no longer rely on investment from the Soviet government, foreign trade and cooperation among Kyrgyzstan's diverse population have become essential to the republic's future success.

CHAPTER THREE

Making
a Living
in Kyrgyzstan

In the distant past, the peoples of Kyrgyzstan hunted, herded animals, and tilled the soil. For most of recorded history, part of the population also earned a living by serving the trading caravans that crossed central Asia. After the region was brought into the Russian Empire in the 1800s, Kyrgyzstan underwent extensive development. Later, Soviet leaders built new factories in Frunze and in other cities to take advantage of Kyrgyzstan's resources.

Despite these changes, Kyrgyzstan remained a very poor republic. In addition, the Soviet Union's system of central economic planning led to inefficiency. Factory managers had little control over production and had no money to spend on modernizing plants. As a result, Kyrgyzstan's outdated businesses now find themselves unable to compete in an open world market.

In Osh, a worker sorts through cocoons, choosing only the best ones for further processing into silk.

The leaders of Kyrgyzstan are planning to sell state-owned industries and to return farmland to private hands. To replace investments that once came from the old Soviet government, the new republic is seeking outside partnerships. With foreign money, Kyrgyz leaders hope to fund the modernization of the country's industries and cities. New investment is slow to arrive, however, a fact that is hampering Kyrgyzstan's economic recovery.

• Agriculture •

A majority of ethnic Kyrgyz still work in agriculture, either by herding livestock or by growing crops. During the 1930s, Kyrgyz herders were forced onto collective farms, but the Kyrgyz government is now disbanding many of these operations. Although they have lost much of their pasture, individual herders are again being allowed to raise their own flocks. Kyrgyz crop farmers struggle with limited precipitation and a short growing season.

A short growing season prevents Kyrgyz farmers from producing a wide variety of crops. Yet the land still yields melons (above) *and corn* (below), *which help to make Kyrgyzstan self-sufficient in food.*

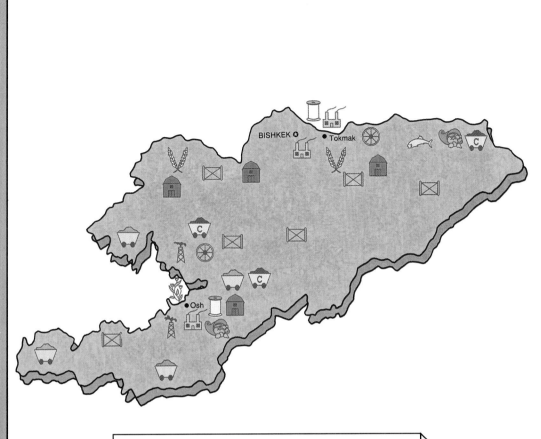

KYRGYZSTAN'S ECONOMIC ACTIVITIES

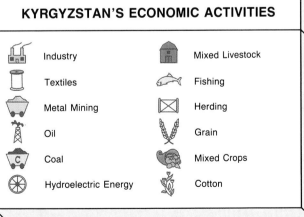

Industry		Mixed Livestock	
Textiles		Fishing	
Metal Mining		Herding	
Oil		Grain	
Coal		Mixed Crops	
Hydroelectric Energy		Cotton	

(Left) **A Kyrgyz woman near Osh milks the family cow. Many rural communities raise livestock for their meat, milk, and hides.** (Below) **An ethnic Uzbek who works in Kyrgyzstan's Fergana Valley spreads freshly picked cotton to dry in the sun.**

Only about 8 percent of Kyrgyzstan's territory is cultivated, much of it with the help of irrigation systems.

About 70,000 Kyrgyz live in the high mountains tending herds of sheep and goats. Other Kyrgyz raise horses, yaks, and goats at lower elevations. About 10 million sheep graze in Kyrgyzstan, making the republic the third largest producer of wool and mutton (sheep meat) in the Commonwealth of Independent States. Along with producing milk and meat, the Kyrgyz also process animal hides into leather goods, such as coats, boots, and gloves.

Many Kyrgyz are employed in the cotton industry, which is centered in the Fergana Valley. The future of cotton growing in central Asia is in doubt because of the environmental damage caused by pesticides. Cotton also requires extensive watering, a practice that is slowly draining the rivers and lakes of central Asia.

(Above) **In north central Kyrgyzstan, a herder guides a large flock to pasture.** (Below) **Some of Kyrgyzstan's raw cotton supplies the nation's textile mills, but most of the crop is exported for final processing into cloth.**

In the past, the Kyrgyz received little benefit from cotton, because almost 80 percent of this crop was shipped to Russia for processing. In the future, the Kyrgyz may be able to earn more by refining their cotton and selling it as finished textiles and clothing. Kyrgyz farmers also grow tobacco, sugar beets, barley, and wheat at altitudes below 5,000 feet (1,500 m). Above that altitude, a short growing season prevents the cultivation of most crops.

Sericulture—the production of raw silk—is a very ancient practice in southern Kyrgyzstan, where workers raise silkworms as well as the mulberry trees on which silkworms feed. The Kyrgyz also collect venom (liquid) from poisonous reptiles. Rare venoms, some of which are more expensive than gold, are added to drugs that are used to treat heart disease.

• Manufacturing, Mining, and Energy •

Nearly all of Kyrgyzstan's manufacturing industries are located in a few cities, including Osh, Bishkek, and Tokmak. Cotton processing takes place in cities near the Fergana Valley, while Bishkek's factories make machinery and farm equipment. A South Korean firm has invested in television and electronics factories in Tokmak. Kyrgyzstan also has smaller industries that produce leather and that package meat.

Kyrgyzstan has extensive mineral resources, including coal, antimony, mercury, zinc, gold, tin, uranium, and lead. Most of these ores, however, are still exported to Russia, where factories process them into finished metals. In addition, many mining jobs are performed by non-Kyrgyz, such as Russians, Ukrainians, and Germans. The emigration of these ethnic groups is causing a shortage of labor in the mining industry.

(Left) **Finished farm equipment waits to be shipped from a factory in Bishkek.** (Below) **At an open-pit mine near Osh, machines dig for coal that lies just below the soil's surface.**

The Soviets built several hydroelectric plants to harness the rapid currents of the Naryn River and other waterways. Many of these plants also hold water in artificial reservoirs. Farmers draw some of this water for irrigation, while the rest powers hydroelectric turbines. These stations reduce the volume of water flowing out of Kyrgyzstan into the river basins beyond the country's borders. As a result, there have been clashes between the central Asian nations over water use.

Other natural resources in Kyrgyzstan include deposits of oil and natural gas, most of which lie in the Fergana Valley. These resources provide almost all of the fossil fuels needed by the republic, but they are also a source of future problems. In combination with the hydroelectric plants along the Naryn River, the mines and factories that exploit minerals and fossil fuels are inefficient and polluting. In addition, these plants will be difficult to operate if skilled laborers choose to emigrate.

• Trade •

Until independence, more than 80 percent of Kyrgyzstan's trade was with the other Soviet republics. Kyrgyzstan now has a severe shortage of money for investment and has limited earnings from foreign trade outside the former Soviet bloc. Many of the country's products, including its mineral resources and agricultural goods, are of low quality and are unattractive to foreign buyers. The Kyrgyz government has plans to develop new technology for converting raw materials into finished goods. This policy would increase Kyrgyzstan's exports and bring in money needed for modernization.

Kyrgyzstan imports vehicles, grain, and chemicals. The nation's principal exports are agricultural

Near the Kazakh border, a recently built dam on the Chu River brings water to Kyrgyz farms. After the central Asian nations broke from the Soviet Union, conflicts erupted over the ownership and use of the region's waterways.

BREWING WATER CONFLICTS

The newly independent republics in central Asia—Kyrgyzstan, Tajikistan, Uzbekistan, Turkmenistan, and Kazakhstan—share many of the same waterways, in particular the Amu Darya and the Syr Darya. These rivers irrigate about 75 percent of the farms in all five republics and provide 52 million central Asians with the water they need for drinking and bathing.

Yet central Asia's vital water supply is drying up while the area's population is rapidly increasing. Each year, more water is taken to irrigate farmland, which has to produce crops to feed more people.

This situation could lead to conflict. Kyrgyzstan, for example, lies upstream and has first access to several rivers, including the Syr Darya. Downstream nations, however, must wait for the rivers to flow to them. Unless the five republics can agree on a fair and efficient way to share scarce water resources, confrontation over water rights seems likely.

Farmers use huge sprinklers to irrigate cropland in northeastern Kyrgyzstan.

At a factory in Osh, a worker arranges newly spun reels of silk thread. Although Kyrgyzstan exports most of its finished silk fabric to Russia, Kyrgyz leaders are seeking additional foreign markets for the valuable cloth.

products, including meat and wool. Kyrgyzstan's silk is exported to Russia, but the Kyrgyz hope to expand this market in the future. Kyrgyzstan has a large trade deficit with other members of the Commonwealth of Independent States. This means that Kyrgyzstan buys more foreign goods than it sells to foreign trading partners.

To stimulate the economy, the Kyrgyz government has opened the nation's industries to foreign investment. In May 1992, for example, Kyrgyzstan signed a **joint venture** agreement with China that provides for direct investment and trade between the two countries. In the same year, the International Monetary Fund approved a grant of money to help the Kyrgyz economy. All the former Soviet republics of central Asia have allied with Iran, Turkey, and Pakistan to establish a regional common market.

CHAPTER FOUR

What's Next for Kyrgyzstan?

The independent Republic of Kyrgyzstan faces political, environmental, social, and economic problems. New political parties—including several based on Islamic principles—are forming within Kyrgyzstan. These groups are pressing for closer ties with Islamic countries, although most Kyrgyz favor a secular government. Disagreements between Islamic and former Communist politicians—a more serious problem in southern Kyrgyzstan—may lead to social tension and even violence.

President Akaev, unlike the heads of most former Soviet republics, never was a Communist party boss. But the Kyrgyz Communists, who have renamed their party the Socialist party, still hold powerful government posts. Despite calls among the Kyrgyz for their resignations, these leaders possess skills and knowledge that will be important in Kyrgyzstan's future.

Since 1991, the Kyrgyz government has established diplomatic relations with many countries, including the United States, which opened its first

Handmade brooms crowd the stall of this vendor in Osh.

INTERNATIONAL WORD GUIDE
ver. 2.1

ENGLISH	KYRGYZ	PRONUNCIATION
Kyrgyzstan	Кыргызстан	kur-gihz-STAHN
Hello	Саламатсызбы	sah-lah-maht SUZZ-buh
Goodbye	Кош	KOSH
Please	Макул	mah-KUHL
Thank you	Ыракмат	uh-rak maht
Yes	Ооба	oh-VAH
No	Жок	JOHK
Good	Жакшы	jahk-SHEE
Bad	Жаман	jah-MAHN

central Asian embassy in Bishkek. Most of the Islamic nations outside the former Soviet Union have also extended recognition to the central Asian states. In April 1992, agreements were reached between Kyrgyzstan, Kazakhstan, Turkmenistan, Uzbekistan, and Tajikistan that provide for closer economic ties and the settlement of border disputes. A more open market in central Asia will help these nations to attract foreign investment and to develop their economies.

Kyrgyzstan is going through a difficult transition that will take many years to be completed. Kyrgyz

On an autumn day, a Russian grandfather reads to his grandson in a Bishkek park.

leaders must build democracy in a nation that has never had elected officials and must establish a free market among businessess that have been under state control for decades. Although Kyrgyzstan has experienced less ethnic and political violence than its neighbors, ethnic tensions remain a threat to the nation's stability. The people of Kyrgyzstan are now taking their first cautious steps together toward a better future.

FAST FACTS
ABOUT KYRGYZSTAN

Total Population	4.5 million
Ethnic Mixture	49 percent Kyrgyz 22 percent Russian 12 percent Uzbek 2 percent Ukrainian 2 percent German
CAPITAL and Major Cities	BISHKEK, Osh
Major Languages	Kyrgyz, Russian
Major Religion	Islam (Sunni branch)
Year of Inclusion in USSR	1936
Status	Fully independent state; member of Commonwealth of Independent States since 1991; joined United Nations in 1992

collective farm: a large agricultural estate worked by a group. The workers usually received a portion of the farm's harvest as wages. On a Soviet collective farm, the central government owned the land, buildings, and machinery.

Commonwealth of Independent States: a union of former Soviet republics that was created by the leaders of Russia, Belarus, and Ukraine in December 1991. The commonwealth has no formal constitution and functions as a loose economic and military association.

Communist: a person who supports Communism—an economic system in which the government owns all farmland and the means of producing goods in factories.

coup d'état: French words meaning "blow to the state" that refer to a swift, sudden overthrow of a government.

Gasoline is scarce in Kyrgyzstan. Truckers bring illegal supplies into the country and sell the fuel on public highways.

Nearly 40 percent of the Kyrgyz population is younger than 15 years of age.

ethnic Kyrgyz: a person whose ethnic heritage is Turkic and who speaks Kyrgyz.

ethnic Russian: a person whose ethnic heritage is Slavic and who speaks Russian.

ethnic Ukrainian: a person whose ethnic heritage is Slavic and who speaks Ukrainian.

glasnost: meaning ''openness,'' the Russian name for a policy of easing restrictions on writing and speaking.

industrialize: to build and modernize factories for the purpose of manufacturing a wide variety of consumer goods and machinery.

joint venture: an economic partnership between a locally owned business and a foreign-owned company.

Illustrations (right and below) *depict episodes in the life of the legendary hero Manas. Preserved in oral form for hundreds of years, the story of Manas was first written down in the 19th century.*

manap: the historic term for a leader of a band of ethnic Kyrgyz from Siberia (eastern Russia).

perestroika: a policy of economic restructuring introduced in the late 1980s. Under perestroika, the Soviet state allowed small, private businesses to form and loosened its control of industry and agriculture.

Russian Empire: a large kingdom that covered present-day Russia as well as areas to the west and south. It existed from roughly the mid-1500s to 1917.

Russian Turkestan: a province of the Russian Empire that covered Kyrgyzstan and the rest of central Asia.

Silk Road: an ancient trade route, linking China and Europe, that passed through Kyrgyzstan and central Asia.

Sufism: a branch of the Islamic faith that was founded in Persia (modern Iran). Sufis worship in private and follow holy mystics.

Union of Soviet Socialist Republics (USSR): a large nation in eastern Europe and northern Asia that consisted of 15 member-republics. It existed from 1922 to 1991.

United Nations: an international organization formed after World War II whose primary purpose is to promote world peace through discussion and cooperation.

• INDEX •

A woman enjoys a traditional Kyrgyz meal, which may include potatoes, mutton (sheep meat), spicy dumplings, and flat loaves of bread.

• *Photo Acknowledgments* •

Photographs used courtesy of: pp. 1, 2, 5, 6, 8 (right), 9, 12 (bottom), 17 (left), 18 (bottom), 19, 20, 22 (left and right), 23, 24, 25 (top and bottom), 26, 32 (left and right), 37, 38, 40, (top and bottom), 42 (left and right), 43 (top and bottom), 44 (bottom), 45, 46, 47, 48, 51, 52, © H. Huntly Hersch; pp. 8 (left), 30, 31, 54 (top and bottom), Independent Picture Service; p. 10, ITAR-TASS/SOVFOTO; p. 12 (top), David Tyson; pp. 13, 36 (bottom), RIA-NOVOSTI/ SOVFOTO; p. 16, © Don Dahler/Stock South; pp. 17 (right), 21, 34 (bottom), 36 (top), 44 (top), TASS/SOVFOTO; pp. 18 (top), 35, 53, 55, Kathleen Kuehnast; p. 33, Poster Collection, RU/SU 1298, Hoover Institution Archives; p. 34 (top), Michael Hamburger. Maps and charts: pp. 14–15, 41, J. Michael Roy; pp. 28–29, 50, 51, Laura Westlund.

Covers: (Front and Back) © H. Huntly Hersch